The Struggles of Being Black:

A Journey Through History And Identity

SAMUEL OWUSU

Copyright © 2025 by SAMUEL OWUSU

All rights reserved. No part of this book may be used or reproduced in any form whatsoever without written permission except in the case of brief quotations in critical articles or reviews.

Printed in the United States of America and or Canada

For more information, or to book an event, contact :
Email -info@cojbookz.com

Book cover design by SAMUEL OWUSU

ISBN: 978-1-998120-79-6

The Struggles of Being Black: A Journey Through History And Identity

Introduction

A brief introduction to the book's purpose: To explore the challenges and triumphs of being Black, examining history, identity, and the ongoing struggles.

A call for empathy and understanding.

"Being Black in this world is both a struggle and a source of immense pride. This journey isn't just a personal experience; it is woven into the fabric of history and society. This book aims to share what it means to walk this path, to face challenges, and to find strength in the face of adversity."

We will explore my opinions with simple text.

CHAPTER 1
A History Of Oppression

Overview of the historical struggles: slavery, colonialism, segregation, and apartheid.

Introduce the generational trauma that still affects Black communities today.

Simple text:

"From the transatlantic slave trade to colonial rule, the history of Black people is a story marked by resilience in the face of dehumanization. The scars of slavery are still visible today in the struggles for justice and equality."

CHAPTER 2
Racism: A Persistent Force

Define racism and its manifestations: systemic, interpersonal, and institutional racism.

Discuss examples of racial discrimination in modern society.

Simple text:

"Racism isn't just something that happens in isolated instances. It is built into systems—schools, workplaces, and healthcare. It's in the way Black bodies are policed, the way history is told, and the way opportunities are denied."

CHAPTER 3
Microaggressions: The Hidden Battle

Talk about everyday occurrences that may seem small but accumulate over time (e.g., assumptions based on skin color, or being treated differently).

- Explain how microaggressions affect mental health and emotional well-being.

Simple text:

"A simple comment, a sideways glance, or a well-meaning but ignorant gesture—these microaggressions are daily reminders of how Black people are still viewed through a lens of 'otherness.' While they may seem small, the toll they take is significant."

CHAPTER 4
Identity And Self-Perception

The struggle of balancing one's cultural heritage and identity with mainstream society's expectations.

The internal conflict of feeling different from both Black and non-Black peers.

Simple text:

"Growing up Black in a predominantly white society often means questioning your place in the world. Am I Black enough? Am I too Black? These questions are part of the journey to understanding who we truly are."

CHAPTER 5
The Struggles Of Black Youth

Focus on the challenges Black children face: stereotypes, academic expectations, and self-esteem issues.

- How young Black children often have to grow up faster due to exposure to racial prejudice.

Simple text:

"Black youth face expectations and stereotypes that shape their futures before they even have the chance to dream. From being called 'too loud' to being told they're 'lazy,' the weight of these words is felt deeply, shaping how they see themselves and the world."

CHAPTER 6
The Fight For Equal Education

The struggles for access to quality education and the achievement gap.

- How educational inequities affect the Black community's future opportunities.

Simple text:

"The fight for educational equity is ongoing. In many communities, Black students attend schools that are underfunded and overlooked, setting them up for failure before they even step foot in a classroom."

CHAPTER 7
The Intersection of Race and Gender

Discuss how Black women and Black men experience racism differently, exploring issues like gender bias, sexism, and the stereotypes surrounding Black femininity and masculinity.

Simple text:

"Being Black and a woman adds another layer to the struggle. From the stereotype of the 'angry Black woman' to the constant struggle for respect in predominantly white spaces, Black women face an intersectional battle that many don't understand."

CHAPTER 8
Police Brutality and the Criminal Justice System

Focus on the disproportionate targeting of Black individuals by law enforcement.

Discuss the systemic issues in the criminal justice system, including mass incarceration and the prison-industrial complex.

Simple text:

"Every Black person has a story, whether personal or from a loved one, of being unjustly profiled or brutalized by the police. The stories of Breonna Taylor, George Floyd, and countless others have become the sad reality of a deeply flawed system."

CHAPTER 9
Black Lives Matter Movement

A deep dive into the Black Lives Matter movement and its significance.

The fight for justice, accountability, and visibility in the face of systemic violence.

Simple text:

"The Black Lives Matter movement gave a voice to the millions who have been silenced by oppression. It was a call for justice, a cry against the status quo, and a demand for a world where Black lives truly matter."

CHAPTER 10
Economic Struggles And Wealth Inequality

The economic disparity between Black and white communities, from employment to housing to generational wealth.

Highlighting how the economic system has been structured to keep Black families from accumulating wealth.

Simple text:

"The economic system is rigged, and Black families are often left behind. From the racial wealth gap to discrimination in the workplace, the struggle for financial stability is harder for Black people, and history has shown that this inequality isn't just a coincidence."

CHAPTER 11
The Role of Family and Community

Discuss the importance of Black families and communities in maintaining cultural identity and providing support in the face of adversity.

- The value of shared experiences and resilience.

Simple text:

"In the face of systemic oppression, Black families and communities serve as pillars of strength. From the family gatherings to the church meetings, these communities are where we find solidarity, love, and hope."

CHAPTER 12
Representation In Media And Entertainment

Explore how Black people are portrayed in the media and the effects of limited or negative representation.

- The growing impact of positive representations in films, television, and music.

Simple text:

"For years, Black people were either invisible or reduced to harmful stereotypes in the media. But now, through the rise of Black directors, actors, and musicians, we're seeing more authentic portrayals that reflect the depth and diversity of the Black experience."

CHAPTER 13
Mental Health and Trauma

Discuss the mental health challenges faced by Black individuals due to racial trauma, discrimination, and societal pressures.

Highlight the importance of seeking mental health care and breaking the stigma.

Simple text:

"The emotional toll of racism is real. It's not just about physical harm; it's about the mental and emotional scars that stay with us long after the incident. Black communities are beginning to recognize the importance of mental health, but it's a journey of healing that's still in progress."

CHAPTER 14
The Importance of Education and Activism

Discuss how education and activism are tools for change.

The legacy of Black leaders and movements that fought for equality and justice.

Simple text:

"The fight for equality is carried forward by those who are willing to speak out, educate, and demand change. From the civil rights movement to today's activists, the voices of Black leaders continue to inspire a movement that demands justice."

CHAPTER 15
Healing and Resilience

Discuss how Black communities continue to heal and fight for justice.

The power of resilience, joy, and celebration of Black culture and identity.

Simple text:

"Despite the ongoing struggles, there is power in resilience. Black people have always found ways to celebrate life through music, dance, art, and love. The culture is one of strength, joy, and resistance."

CHAPTER 16
The Future: Hope For Change

Focus on the optimism for a better future where equality and justice are possible.

The role that the next generation plays in shaping a more inclusive world.

Simple text:

"The future is shaped by the work we do today. As the world becomes more interconnected and diverse, there is hope for a future where Black lives are valued, celebrated, and treated with the dignity they deserve."

CHAPTER 17
Conclusion: A Call For Action

End with a powerful message about the importance of allyship and continuing the fight for justice.

A call for everyone to contribute to making a world free of racism and inequality.

Simple text:

The struggles of being Black are not just the responsibility of Black people to fight. We all have a role to play in dismantling racism, fighting injustice, and creating a world where equality is not just a dream but a reality. The journey continues, and we must all walk it together."

Acknowledgments

I want to sincerely thank Kamelah Blair and The My Black Is Whole Program for their guidance, encouragement, and belief in my journey as a writer. Your leadership and dedication have left a lasting impact on me, not only through your individual support but also through the powerful work you both do within the mentorship organization.

To the entire team behind the mentorship program — thank you for creating a space where young voices are nurtured, challenged, and uplifted. This opportunity to write and share my story has been deeply meaningful, and it would not have been possible without the foundation you've built.

Your commitment to cultivating creativity, confidence, and purpose in emerging writers is something I will always carry with me. I'm grateful for the chance to be part of this experience and the door you opened that allowed this book to be written.

NOTES

The Struggles of Being Black: A Journey Through History And Identity

SAMUEL OWUSU

The Struggles of Being Black: A Journey Through History And Identity

SAMUEL OWUSU

www.ingramcontent.com/pod-product-compliance
Lightning Source LLC
Chambersburg PA
CBHW051714090426
42736CB00013B/2702